CCSS **Genre** Expository Text

W9-AXM-219

Essential Question
What are features of different animal habitats?

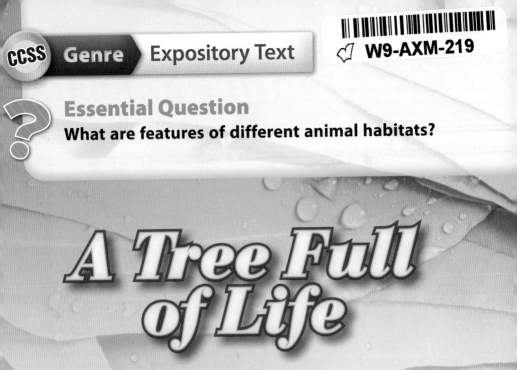

A Tree Full of Life

by Susan Evento

CHAPTER 1

Eucalyptus Forests

A tree stands tall in the heart of a forest. It is one of many eucalyptus (yew-kuh-LIP-tuhs) trees in many eucalyptus forests in Australia. This giant tree is a habitat, or home, to lots of animals. They depend on the eucalyptus to meet their needs.

KEY
● Eucalyptus forests

Indian Ocean

Coral Sea

AUSTRALIA

Tasmania

The continent of Australia has many eucalyptus forests.

Eucalyptus trees may be extremely tall. Some eucalyptus trees can climb above 300 feet! This tree has been standing for many years. Its mighty trunk has sticky bark that hangs like string. Its leaves smell sweet and spicy. Its flowers and fruit do, too.

Although eucalyptus leaves are sweet, they are also poisonous!

CHAPTER 2

Food for Animals

It is a warm summer night, and the sky is bright with stars. A hungry koala bear sits up high in the branches of this tree. It spends hours chewing the tree's leaves. It takes a long time to eat an entire pound of them! The leaves have water, but they aren't very **nutritious**. The koala needs to eat a lot of leaves to get the vitamins it needs.

After the koala chews the eucalyptus leaves into a mush, its stomach can break down their poisons.

DID YOU KNOW?

- Koala bears are not bears. They are **marsupials**, animals with pouches.
- Koala bears smell like cough drops because of the sweet leaves they eat.
- Koala bears have been known to jump from tree to tree.

The mother koala snuggles with the baby, or joey.

The tired koala finally falls asleep. It sleeps wedged between branches with the baby koala resting peacefully in its arms. The koala bear sleeps through most of the day. In fact, it may not wake up for 18 hours.

The koala isn't on the ground much because it isn't safe from other animals, such as dingoes.

The koala finally awakes and climbs down the tree. It doesn't go on a journey. It moves to the next eucalyptus tree that smells good. The eucalyptus tree has everything the koala will need for a while. It gives food and water. It also gives **shelter**, which is a place to sleep.

The koala climbs up high in the branches of the new tree. It chews the tasty leaves. Now it has found a new resting place where it will stay for a while.

The koala is not the only animal that depends on the eucalyptus tree for food. Other animals eat different parts of the tree. For example, thousands of termites are buried within the bark. They are chewing away at the tree's hard covering. At last they are full. They have eaten away parts of the trunk and branches.

These tiny termites have strong mouth parts for eating wood.

Termite nests are sometimes built in the shape of a mound.

The eucalyptus bark provides food for the termites. But that is not the only thing the bark is good for. The termites chew the bark a lot, which turns it into a paste. Then the hungry termites eat the paste. They also use it to build nests. The paste is like a strong glue that holds the nest together. Termite babies will live in these nests.

CHAPTER 3

Shelter for Animals

Now the termites have chewed holes in this tree. These empty spaces make wonderful nests for other animals.

"Ha, ha, ha, ha." This funny sound comes from a kookaburra (KOOK-uh-BUR-ruh) bird. This bird peeks out of its nest and spies an enemy below. Then it quickly drops back inside. It will be safe hiding inside the tree.

Because of its unusual sound, the kookaburra is called the laughing bird.

Next, a sugar glider flies toward the eucalyptus tree. Like the koala, it depends on the tree for food. The sugar glider stops to eat the tree's sweet sap. Then it enters its nest. It joins its babies for a rest.

Sugar gliders enjoy a nest in a hollow made by termites.

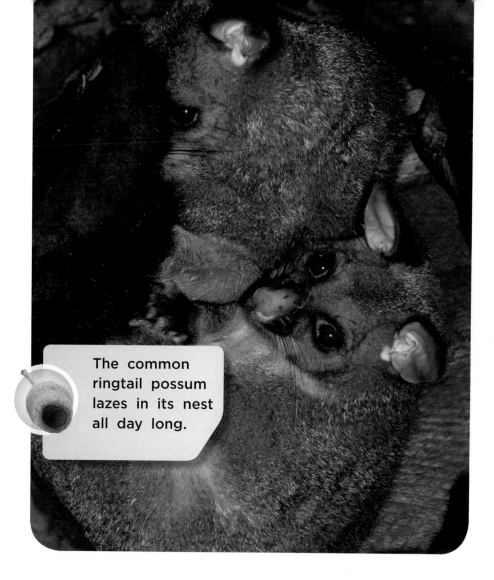

The common ringtail possum lazes in its nest all day long.

The common ringtail possum hangs from a branch. It hangs by its hairless tail! It depends on the eucalyptus tree for food and shelter. It eats the leaves and flowers of this tree. The possum collects bark and grass. These **materials** are used to line its nest. Like the koala, it is busy at night.

Wombats can run fast and dive into hidden tunnels when enemies chase them.

A wombat crawls along the forest floor. It eats eucalyptus leaves and roots it finds on the ground. It does this for hours each night. Then it escapes into its underground tunnel. Much like the koala, the wombat sleeps away the day.

CHAPTER 4
Tree of Life

Most of the fruit bats in Australia are called grey-headed flying foxes.

It grows dark. The fruit bats become restless. They fly to the eucalyptus tree to eat its **pollen** and fruit. They fly from tree to tree. In this way they spread pollen. This helps new eucalyptus trees grow. Plants and animals work together in nature.

This drooping mistletoe plant provides food for both the mistletoe bird and a butterfly.

It is not just animals who depend on the life-giving eucalyptus tree. Plants live in this tree, too. It provides food as well as shelter. This mistletoe plant lives far up in its highest branches. It eats the sap of the eucalyptus tree. Mistletoe birds then eat the fruit of the plant. The eucalyptus tree is full of life!

Respond to Reading

Summarize

Use the important details to summarize *A Tree Full of Life*.

Main Topic		
Detail	Detail	Detail

Text Evidence

1. How do you know that *A Tree Full of Life* is narrative nonfiction? Identify the text features. **GENRE**

2. In what ways are eucalyptus trees helpful to animals? Use details from the selection to support your answer. **MAIN TOPIC AND KEY DETAILS**

3. Use your knowledge of suffixes to figure out the meaning of *wonderful* on page 14. **SUFFIXES**

4. Write about how termites use eucalyptus trees. Use story details to support your answer. **WRITE ABOUT READING**

Compare Texts
How are the features of a eucalyptus tree and a
termite mound different?

Life in a Termite Mound

Imagine the strange world of a
termite mound. Termites chew
wood to make paste. Then
they mix it with mud. They use
these materials to build a nest.
Sometimes these nests reach over
12 feet tall! Some have millions of
termites living in them.

Termites are excellent nest builders.

Inside the Mound

The mound is made up of many
small rooms. There are rooms
called **nurseries**. The nurseries are
where the eggs hatch. The young
termites grow up in these rooms.

**The inside of a termite mound
looks like a sponge.**

egg

Jobs in the Colony

A king and queen termite start a **colony**, or group, of termites. The queen lays many eggs in the nest. There are many worker termites in a colony. They collect food and feed the young. They also build and take care of the nest. Soldier termites protect the colony.

Termites	Duties
king and queen	start colony
queen	lay eggs
workers	build/take care of nests collect food feed young
soldiers	protect nests

Make Connections

How would you describe the different parts of a termite mound? ESSENTIAL QUESTION

How are eucalyptus trees and termite mounds alike? TEXT TO TEXT

Glossary

colony *(KOL-uh-nee)* a group of termites *(page 18)*

marsupials *(mahr-SEW-pee-uhlz)* animals with pouches *(page 4)*

materials *(muh-TEER-ee-uhls)* things used to build or make something *(page 11)*

nurseries *(NUR-suh-reez)* rooms in termite mounds where eggs hatch and grow *(page 17)*

nutritious *(new-TRISH-uhs)* useful as a food *(page 4)*

pollen *(PAWL-uhn)* a yellow powder that fertilizes *(page 13)*

shelter *(SHEL-tuhr)* something that covers or protects *(page 6)*

Index

Focus on Science

Purpose To find out about the different features of a habitat

What to Do

 Step 1 Think about the different animals that live in and around eucalyptus trees in Australia.

 Step 2 Draw a chart like this one.

Animal	Where They Live in Tree	Part of Tree They Eat

Step 3 Fill it in with information from the text.

Conclusion Choose one animal from your chart. Draw a picture of it. Include the food it eats and where it lives in the tree. Share your drawing with a partner. Then discuss what you have learned.